MERCEN

Mercenaries:

"Counter-Insurgency" in the Gulf

Fred Halliday

SPOKESMAN

First Published in 1977

This book is copyright under the Berne Convention. All rights are reserved. Apart from any fair dealing for the purpose of private study, research, criticism or review, as permitted under the Copyright Act, 1956, no part of this publication may be reproduced, stored in a retrieval system, or transmitted, in any form or by any means, electronic, electrical, chemical, mechanical, optical, photocopying, recording or otherwise, without the prior permission of the copyright owner. Enquiries should be addressed to the publishers.

Paper ISBN 0 85124 197 2

Copyright © Fred Halliday

Published by the Bertrand Russell Peace Foundation Ltd., Bertrand Russell House, Gamble Street, Nottingham for *Spokesman*

Printed by the Russell Press Ltd., Nottingham

Acknowledgements

The following study of counter-insurgency in Oman was first published by the Gulf Committee, London, in May 1976. Work on the original study and on this revised material was made possible by a grant from the Third World Project of the Transnational Institute, Amsterdam.

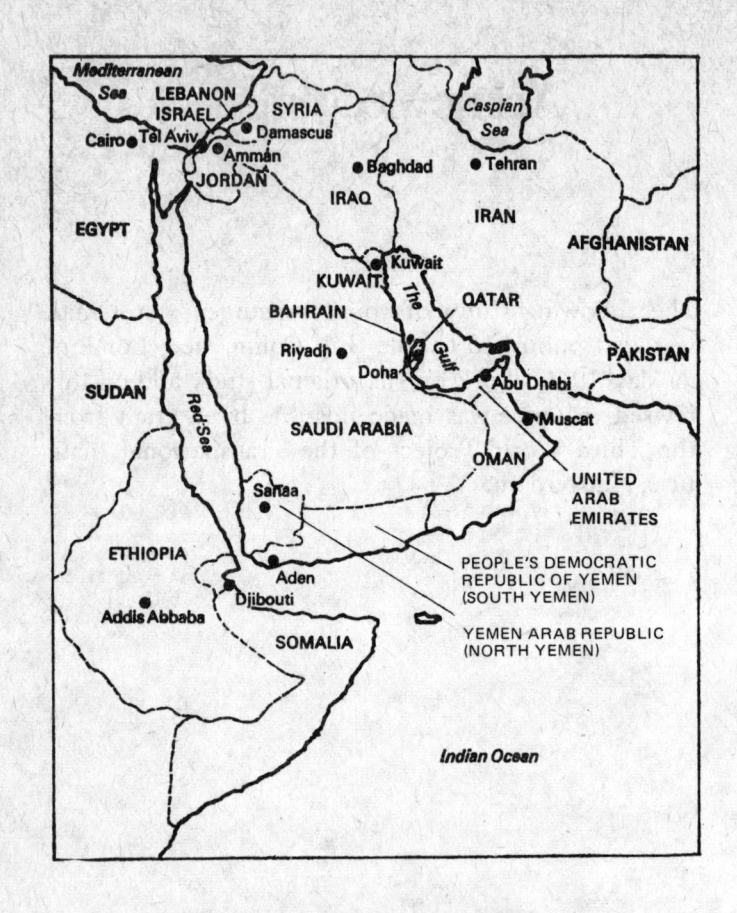

The Arabian Peninsula

Contents

I   British Mercenaries and
Counter-Insurgency in the
Middle East   9

II   Counter-Insurgency Old and New:
The Case of Oman   24

    Appendices   69

British Mercenaries and Counter-Insurgency in the Middle East

It was the Angolan War of 1975-1976 and the subsequent trial of captured British citizens that re-focused attention on the question of British mercenaries, and on the factors in British society that encourage people to volunteer to fight in this way. The trial of the mercenaries is now over. A British government Commission has met and presented its report. But the matter is far from dead. Those who organised the Angola mercenaries have not been touched, or even properly identified. The majority of those who went out to kill have not been brought to justice. Moreover, we can only expect that as the fighting in southern Africa intensifies in the next months or years so the demand for mercenaries will increase.

It is not, however, only in Africa that British mercenaries are used, nor is this probably the main area of their activity. In the Middle East, and specifically in the oil-rich states of the Arabian Peninsula, British mercenaries of various kinds have been used for a long time, and their continued use there is essential to maintaining the anti-democratic system that prevails in the region. This use of British mercenaries in

Arabia was indeed mentioned at the time of the Angolan war. John Banks, one of the main recruiters of mercenaries in Britain, pointed out several times that it was inconsistent for people to criticise mercenaries going to Angola when the British government encouraged ex-servicemen to fight as mercenaries in Oman. And, in the recommendations of the Diplock Committee set up by the British government after the Angolan affair, it was explicitly recognised that the govenment should retain the right to decide which countries mercenaries could, and could not, go to fight in. The moral is evident enough: the British government is not opposed to mercenaries as such, only to people fighting in wars of which the government disapproves.

The Middle East oil producers of the more conservative kind are probably the most obvious example of countries which are permitted to recruit British military personnel. This has been true for decades, but far from being a relic of the past it is something that has increased in scale in recent years in response to the new situation in these states. In the first place, British military personnel have been directly involved in helping the monarchs of the region to crush opposition forces that have arisen. Secondly, these rulers have become the largest purchasers of arms in the world since the rise in the price of oil in 1971-1973 and the acquisition of these arms has gone together with an inflow of thousands of western military personnel into the area.

The interest of the British government here is evident enough. Britain was long the dominant colonial power in the Gulf region and wants to ensure that the pro-western regimes in the area, guarding two-thirds of the world's oil reserves, remain in power. A considerable British presence, military, political and economic, has remained, despite the formal withdrawal of British forces in 1971. At the same time the British government sees the increased oil revenues as an opportunity to sell more arms and to boost British exports, and with the arms go the personnel.

Since 1966 the main promoter of British arms exports has been the Ministry of Defence's *Defence Sales Organisation*. Arms exports have risen from £150 millions in 1966 to £560 millions in the financial year 1975-1976, and will possibly exceed £800 millions in 1976-1977. Britain lags behind three other competitors in this field, but the promotion of arms exports, especially to the Gulf region, has become a major part of this country's export drive. Among the most important arms contracts signed in recent years have been: a contract to sell 1,200 Chieftain tanks to Iran, and another 165 to Kuwait; contracts to sell Rapier anti-aircraft missiles to Iran, Abu Dhabi, Oman and Saudi Arabia; a contract to sell 12 Jaguar jets to Oman. British salesmen have indeed hoped for much more: during the visit to Britain of Saudi Defence and Aviation Minister Prince Sultan in November 1976 there was much (officially-inspired) speculation in the press about him ordering arms worth £3,000 millions. As it turned out he was only prepared, at that stage, to renew the existing contract with the British Aircraft Corporation to service and maintain the Saudi airforce. This was worth, however, some £760 millions over four years.

It cannot be stated often enough that all these monarchs — Iranian, Saudi, Kuwaiti, Omani, and the rest — are extremely conservative and repressive rulers. In none of these countries is any opposition allowed. The working class has no right to organise independently or to strike. Women are still subjected to sustained and degrading oppression. The arms being sent out, and the personnel that accompany them, are being used to consolidate regimes of this kind. We know too from recent revelations that the trade in arms has been accompanied by corruption on a hitherto undreamt-of scale. Whilst most attention has focused on the activities of US firms such as Lockheed and Northrop, British firms are also involved. A Lieutenant-Colonel in the Royal Corps of Signals, David Randel, was arrested in April 1976 on charges of corruption in connection with the sale of telecommunications equipment to the Oman. Earlier, in 1971, a British officer who had served in the Middle East, brought an action against BAC salesman Geoffrey Edwards on the grounds that the latter had promised him commissions of 5 per cent and 10 per cent on all BAC sales to Arab countries and had till then given him only £40,000.[2] These are almost certainly only the tip of the iceberg.

The sale of British arms overseas to boost counter-revolutionary governments is not, of course, confined to the Gulf. British sales to South Africa are on a par with those to Iran and the Arab monarchies, and have correspondingly increased in recent years as the situation in southern Africa has intensified. The 1976 report *Black South Africa Explodes*, published by Counter Information Services in London, details the activities of four such firms: Plessey, who manufacture in South Africa integrated circuits, a component of sophisticated weapons systems; Racal Electronics, the world's largest supplier of radio manpacks and tank radios, and one of the most profitable firms on the London Stock Exchange in 1976; Marconi, who are building an £8 millions 'tropospheric scatter system' as part of a computer-controlled communication system; and ICI, who through African Explosives and Chemical Industries Ltd., in which it has a 40% interest, manufactures teargas, nerve gas and defoliants. Marconi and Racal are both active in, for example, Oman where they have participated in building up the communications and air defence systems.

This trade in arms is not however the only way in which Britain is helping the monarchs of the Gulf to keep themselves in power. Part of the co-operation involves the provision by Britain of help in counter-insurgency and Special Branch work. As is examined in what follows, Britain probably has the widest experience and expertise in this kind of repressive activity, and which, whilst to some extent based on colonial war, is still of relevance to many governments throughout the world. Within the past year alone it is possible to identify a number of countries that have put British policy to their own uses. In both Malaya and Rhodesia, the local governments are facing growing armed popular resistance and have resorted to the traditional British techniques of food control and population regroupment to try to separate the guerrilla forces from their popular base.[3] Moreover, the Portuguese in Mozambique and the USA in Vietnam drew on this reserve of British experience.

The British Army's continuing involvement in Northern Ireland is also providing relevant experience to many of Britain's allies. Belfast provides the most advanced and protracted case of urban armed conflict in an industrialised country that has ever been seen. Nothing in France (in the late 1950s) or in West Germany or the USA more recently compares with the past few years in Ulster. Nor has any counter-guerrilla campaign in any Latin American country reached the scale of that seen in Northern Ireland. It is not surprising therefore that other governments are quietly but carefully learning from this experience, just as the regional police forces in Britain are also ensuring that their senior officers have acquaintance with the kinds of operations undertaken by the Ulster force.

Two examples from 1976 will also illustrate how foreign governments are learning from Northern Ireland: following the upsurge of West Bank Palestinian resistance to Israeli occupation in the spring of 1976, the Israeli government let it be known that 'the Army may adopt methods similar to those used by the British Army in Northern Ireland'.[4] After the suppression of the 'attempted leftist coup' in Portugal in November 1975, NATO helped to rebuild the counter-revolutionary security forces. *The Times* reported that 'Officers in the new riot police, for example, have received advice from the police in London and from two British officers at Thiepval Barracks in Northern Ireland'[5]

We do not have information on the numbers of British personnel involved in diffusing this kind of information, nor on the numbers of foreign personnel that have received training in British counter-insurgency techniques. However, we do have general figures on military co-operation between Britain and other states. In January 1976 military personnel from no less than 66 other countries were training in Britain, whilst in the period 1971-1975 British armed forces personnel served on loan and as instructors with 33 foreign armies. Not all of these personnel, probably not the majority, were involved in the diffusion of counter-insurgency information and techniques. But a significant number certainly were; and, just as control and repression techniques have come to play a more important part in courses for British officers in recent years (e.g. at Sandhurst), so one can expect that foreign interest in, and need for, these techniques have also grown.

In the Middle East, arms sales, mercenaries, and counter-insurgency have all gone together. Rich, repressive and vulnerable governments have turned to Britain, as well as to the USA and France, for the techniques they need. Within this general flow of arms and 'advice', large numbers of service and ex-service personnel are involved. Most are in some way mercenaries — i.e. providing military skills for payment — and precisely because of the complex character of the current relationship it is important to distinguish between the different kinds of mercenary now active in the region. At least five distinct kinds can be identified.

1. The popular image of a mercenary is of the soldier who fights an undercover war for a high payment. This image is especially that of the mercenary in Africa — in Angola, and before that in the Congo. In Arabia, mercenaries of this kind were active in the North Yemeni civil war in the 1960s. Britain and Saudi Arabia supported the royalist tribes fighting the

Egyptian-backed republican forces. The dozens of British mercenaries sent in were used for three functions: training, specialised offensive operations, communications. The main British front man for the campaign was Colonel David Stirling, founder of the SAS regiment, and in 1975 notorious as the head of a right-wing private army, GB 75. However, the real point about this operation was that it was backed by the British government in order to counter Egyptian pressure on the British position in Aden.[6] It was a deliberate attempt to overthrow a government of which Britain disapproved, but where Britain did not want to be seen to intervene directly.

2. Closely related to these mercenaries are the soldiers who work with governments for the pay. Ex-British service personnel have served in the Arabian Peninsula for decades — in the army and air force, in defence administration, and in the police, Special Branch and intelligence divisions. In the small state of Qatar, for example, enormous power was held until 1972 by two legendary figures: one, an ex-Glasgow policeman named Ronald Cochrane, had adopted the Muslim name of Mohammad Mahdi, and headed the army, whilst the other, Ronald Lock, headed the police. In the neighbouring state of Bahrain, the Special Branch is still run by a mysterious officer called Henderson. A similar pattern holds in the armies and police forces of the United Arab Emirates, where dozens of British mercenaries are employed. However, the most spectacular case of mercenary employment has been and remains the Sultanate of Oman. Here hundreds of mercenaries have manned the army, air force and navy, and in the decade after 1965 were involved in the counter-insur-

gency operation against guerrillas in the southern, Dhofar, province of the country. In an interview with ITV in 1972 the commander of the Dhofar gendarmerrie, Major Ray Barker-Scofield praised Dhofar as 'the last place in the world where an Englishman is still called sahib', and explained his role as follows: 'I am a mercenary and a professional soldier and I've done twenty-five years abroad in such places as India, Burma, South Africa, Egypt, Somalia, Mogadishu, Libya and Germany. This is my profession. Basically I am on the market'. Here, as in North Yemen, the mercenaries work with the approval of the British government. They are indeed under the command of a serving British officer, since each branch of the Sultan's armed forces is commanded by such a regular soldier.

3. The officers seconded from the British services to the Middle East armed forces are also in essence mercenaries. Whilst they themselves may not see it this way, they are hired out by the British government as part of the policy of getting money from oil states, and the Ministry of Defence makes a profit on the deal. According to one report, London hires officers to the Sultan of Oman for *twice* the rate these officers are paid.[7] The provision of these soldiers is directly related to arms sales and/or counter-insurgency operations: in the 1970s the two regions where most officers of this kind have gone are the Gulf and South-East Asia. In both areas guerrilla operations (Oman, Malaya, Brunei) or sustained repression (Iran, Kuwait, Amirates, Singapore) have been the norm. Recent figures for the Gulf indicate the continued role of British seconded personnel:

	1971	1972	1973	1974	1975	1976
Iran	21	48	36	62	71	74
Oman	92	121	154	170	235	216
Kuwait	106	112	112	118	118	118
Emirates	121	105	77	53	43	44

In 1977 there are over 140 British personnel in Kuwait, part of a "Kuwait Liaison Team", that is training the 9,000-Kuwait army in the use of tanks, and in fact acting as an expert backbone to the whole Kuwait military apparatus. The presence has been especially strong in Oman, where regular British personnel have fallen into at least three categories. First, they have commanded, officered and trained the local armed forces. These have been officers and technicians from the three services. The figures above cover only *this* group.[8] Secondly, the Special Air Services regiment has had a detachment in Oman since 1971: disguised as a British Army Training Team, it has carried out offensive operations, whilst at the same time training local counter-guerrilla groups and organising 'hearts and minds' campaigns. Thirdly, several hundred British service personnel were deployed guarding and servicing the two RAF bases at Salala and Masirah, which were to be handed over to Oman at the end of March 1977.

Despite the formal withdrawal from Oman, the UK presence remains very strong, and the Sultan's main advisers include a number of powerful and suspicious British operatives. Some visitors to Oman suggest that real power in the Sultanate is indeed wielded by a shadowy duo of British "advisers". One is Tim Landen, an army Captain, who studied with the Sultan at Sandhurst, organised the 1970 coup that brought the Sultan to power, and has since been the latter's right-hand-man, officially his aide-de-camp. The other is Tony Ashworth, an intelligence official active in Aden during the emergency there, and for a time head of the British "information" office in Hong Kong. He is formally "on secondment" to the Ministry of Information (see later p.61-2). The official British policy is to play down the importance of these two sinister people, but those in Oman are well aware of the influence they have.

4. In addition to these three kinds of British personnel, there are thousands working on arms contracts in the region — training, installing and manning British-exported equipment. They are part of the growing local military establishments. Precise figures are not available, but the British Aircraft Corporation have had around 2,000 personnel in Saudi Arabia since 1965, and hundreds of other British technicians are now in Iran, Kuwait, Oman and the smaller Gulf states. Although not directly involved in fighting, they are performing a major military role: their very presence acts as a deterrent to other states and some of the pilots supplied by BAC to Saudi Arabia in the mid-1960s did fly operational missions along the Saudi border with North Yemen. Given the dependence of these states on foreign technicians to install and operate the new arms for years to come, it would be quite unrealistic to rule out the possibility that some would be used, in the front line or in backup roles, for military operations. The very pileup of arms makes such conflicts more likely, and the number of foreign personnel is increasing. The most marked case of this is in Iran where by 1980 there are going to be 60,000

US expatriates and their families, most of them working on defence-related contracts. But in Saudi Arabia and the other Arab states the British presence is substantial and will continue. Some idea of the diversity of the operations in which British personnel are engaged outside of the traditional British colonies can be gauged from studying the case of Iran. Whilst we do not have a full breakdown of what is happening, the following distinct items can be identified:

a. The British Aircraft Corporation is planning to help the Iranians build Rapier missiles in Iran, as part of a £400 millions oil-for-arms arrangement. An unknown number of British technicians will be involved in setting up and then maintaining the necessary installations.

b. Britain is supplying the Iranian Army with a special kind of tank armour, Chobham armour, to be used on the 1,200 Chieftain Tanks the Shah has under order. The British Army's own tanks in Germany will not receive this equipment for some time after the Iranian army has acquired it. Further personnel will be sent out to install and probably service these tanks.

c. In an unpublicised arrangement, a unit of the counter-guerrilla SAS regiment has for some time been training Iranian soldiers. Since March 1974 Cambridge University has been teaching groups of 6 SAS Persian language, with special emphasis on military vocabulary. What the SAS are up to in Iran is not clear, but they are no doubt playing some role in the buildup of Iran's own counter-insurgency forces, for use both outside Iran (as in Oman and Pakistan) and inside, against the Shah's own people.

d. British firms are helping the Iranian police to build up a new computerised information and communications system. In 1975 the Iranian police's communications division sent 15 volumes of specifications to the British government-run sales organisation, Millbank Technical Services. Estimates of the contract's possible worth ran up to £100 millions. Firms involved in initial planning include Racal, Cable and Wireless, Laing and Wimpey; although the final arrangements have not been made, Iranian police are already being trained in both Britain and Iran by British personnel.

None of these projects is, of course, designed to further the development of economic prosperity or freedom in Iran. They are designed to strengthen the repressive system on which the Shah relies, and, in the case of the armour and missiles, to threaten Iran's neighbours. It is in this kind of operation that the British experts and advisers are participating, and which has made Iran the purchaser of 60% of all Britain's arms exports.

5. No discussion of mercenaries would be complete without focusing on the most numerous kind of mercenary in the region — the poor. These are not British or American, but impoverished peasants from the less fortunate countries of the region: peasants from North Yemen, nomads from Pakistani Baluchistan, Pathans, Dhofaris. Historically many of the local rulers preferred to recruit via middlemen from outside their own area, and the expansion of local armed forces has continued this trend. Probably 40 per cent of the Sultan of Oman's 12,000 strong army is Baluchi.

It is a sad feature of the situation in the Middle East that so many thousands of these men, without any ideological motive, have been driven by hunger to fight and suppress their class counterparts in other states.

The most extreme case of British counter-insurgency and of the use of mercenaries is undoubtedly Oman, where a regular British services presence, backed by mercenaries and British arms salesmen, has helped to crush the armed resistance of the people and keep the autocratic Sultan in power. The following study, a revised version of an essay published a year ago, tries to relate the Dhofar war to the wider experience of British counter-insurgency and to the changes that have been taking place in the Gulf region over the past decade. At the same time it identifies the different ways in which British forces have been used and their co-operation with other armies in Oman.

The lessons of Oman are two-fold. First, that with the decline of old-style colonialism, wars of counter-revolution will tend to be fought by *coalitions* of powers, rather than by individual states. Secondly, as part of this internationalisation, the lessons learnt by one nation, in this case Britain, will be learnt by other states who may be able to use them in situations that the British Army no longer confronts. The British Empire may be all but gone, but the role of Britain — government, services and arms companies — in counter-revolution and counter-insurgency throughout the world is still a considerable one. Indeed, the demand for assistance from Britain in these fields has probably grown. Socialists have therefore a continuing, if not increased, duty to reveal and oppose activities of this kind.

FOOTNOTES
1. US sales in 1974 were £4,200 millions, the Soviet Union's £2,250 m. and France's £1,500 m. (*Sunday Times*, 25 April 1976).
2. *The Observer*, 10 October 1971. By his own reckoning the man involved, a Colonel Richard Lonsdale, was entitled to commission on 8 deals totalling £313 millions.
3. Rhodesian use of these techniques is well documented in *Racial Discrimination and Repression in Southern Rhodesia*, published by the International Commission of Jurists and the Catholic Institute for International Relations, 1976.
4. *The Times*, 19 May 1976.
5. *The Times*, 28th May 1976.
6. For details see my *Arabia without Sultans*, (London, 1974) pp. 140 and 149 note 10, and David Smiley (one of the organisers) *Arabian Assignment* (London, 1975).
7. *Sunday Times*, 16 July 1972.
8. The official British figures for personnel in Oman also included only the first category and excluded the others on the grounds that they were not officially seconded to the local armies — an artificial distinction.

*Since this study went to press, three additional books relating to the topics under discussion have appeared. *The Technology of Political Control*, by Carol Ackroyd, Karen Margolis, Jonathan Rosenhead, and Tim Shallice (Penguin Books, 1977), provides the most detailed analysis yet made of the latest British counter-insurgency techniques. Anthony Sampson's *The Arms Bazaar* provides a comprehensive account of the arms trade with the Middle East, and the British arms export business. *Oman: The Making of the Modern State* by John Townsend, former economic adviser to the Sultanate of Oman, is an interesting inside account of the first years of Sultan Qabus' rule.

Counter-Insurgency Old and New: The Case of Oman[1]

The war in Oman, which began in 1965 in Dhofar, the southern province of that country, and lasted for over a decade was characterised by two paradoxes. First of all, it was in one sense a small-scale and obscure conflict, involving relatively few people in a remote mountain region. Very little was ever heard about it, in the Middle East or elsewhere. Yet this was no backyard police operation: far more than Vietnam or any war in Africa or Latin America, it affected control of a major economic asset of the capitalist world — Gulf oil.[2] Although to a certain extent the result of its scale, the obscurity that surrounded the war was also the result of a deliberate policy of concealing, or at least minimising, its significance; and the apparent insignificance was eloquently contradicted by the fact that, although Britain was initially the sole outside party involved, the conflict in Dhofar became a highly *internationalised* one, in which at least nine foreign powers participated in the campaigns to crush the guerrillas. The participation of these powers is illustrative not only of the fact that the suppression of the Dhofar guerrillas was essential to the region's stability, but also of a new inter-state system being built in the Gulf. A second characteristic paradox follows from this, namely that the war in Dhofar *combined* elements of a traditional British colonial war with those of a post-colonial counter-insurgency operation, of a kind that is likely to recur in the last quarter of the 20th Century. It was therefore probably the last of the old campaigns and, while not the first, one of the first half-dozen of the new, simultaneously a retrospective on a century of British colonial control and an index of some of what is to come.

The apparent military consolidation of the counter-revolutionary forces in Oman in 1975 stands in contrast to the overall record of that year, which is to a considerable degree one of triumph for revolutionary guerrilla movements. In Indochina the US and their allies fled as Cambodia, Vietnam and finally Laos fell to the popular forces. In Africa the independent states of Mozambique and Guinea-Bissau were established in the wake of the Portuguese retreat; by the end of the year, even in Angola, the MPLA after an uncertain start was well on the way to controlling the whole country with Cuban support. In a number of other states — in Malaya, Iran, Palestine, the Basque country, Eritrea, Chad, Namibia, Zimbabwe, Argentina — guerrillas of various political characters, operating in many kinds of social and geographical contexts, were able at least to continue their operations. Elsewhere it *was* a different story: in Portugal's East Indian colony, Timor, the under-equipped FRETILIN forces were driven into the mountains by an Indonesian invasion, and in Oman the Sultan and his foreign supporters were able to impose control on most of the Dhofar province; while some guerrillas remained in central and eastern Dhofar, the majority took up defensive positions across the border, in South Yemen.

In addition to describing the counter-insurgency tactics used, the analysis provided here will attempt to assess the balance of forces operating in Dhofar, to identify the determining objective forces. This is necessary, especially since guerrilla war is often a very costly and unpleasant form of revolutionary struggle. Despite the record of 1975, it has in most cases been defeated. We are now a long way from the triumphalist rhetoric of the mid-1960s, from the Che Guevara's 'two, three, many Vietnams' and Lin Piao's villages encircling the towns on a global scale. The USA has developed and diffused a new technology and theory of counter-insurgency which has had its successes: in Latin America, except to some extent Argentina, every rural and urban guerrilla movement, including the Tupamaros, has been defeated. In India and Zaire, two hopes of the 60s, the revolutionary movements have been at least temporarily crushed; whilst in Indonesia and Chile the left has had no effective reply, guerrilla or otherwise, to the Army's overthrow of the progressive regimes. As we shall see, the record of British colonialism since 1945 has also been disturbingly successful on the military level at least.

The New Order in the Gulf

The new system or order taking shape in the Gulf is intended to effect the transitions and resolve the tensions that began in the late 1950s; by 1975 the main components of the new order were established.[3] Four main points can be identified:

1. Decolonisation:

Until the mid-1950s Britain dominated most of the Arabian coastline, and maintained a predominant influence in Iraq. Only Saudi Arabia and Iran, monarchies under US influence, and North Yemen, the only truly independent Arabian state, remained outside British control. A military coup ousted British influence in Iraq in 1958; in 1961 Kuwait became independent, whilst a decade later three other small Gulf states followed (Bahrain, Qatar, the United Arab Emirates). The two most difficult cases were South Yemen and Oman. In the former, Britain failed to sustain the government of its choosing and had to hand over power to the nationalist guerrilla movement, the National Liberation Front, in 1967. In the latter Britain never admitted to having a colonial position, and the change here was therefore more implicit and gradual: in fact in contrast to Oman's allegedly non-colonial status, that country has remained the one where the British position is strongest, but where Iran has acquired a powerful position in the early 1970s. The US hold in Saudi Arabia and Iran was by contrast always informal and not colonial in any strict sense of that term: the evolution of these two states from the mid-1960s onwards, with the Shah's white revolution and King Feisal's modernisation, has made them stronger and more independent entities.

2. Containing Revolution:

Two major threats to the establishment of a new order in the Gulf began with the Iraqi coup of 1958 and the North Yemeni coup of 1962. The former undermined the Baghdad Pact — Baghdad being the capital of Iraq the organisation had to be renamed the Central Treaty Organisation.[4] For a decade and a half, the succession of military juntas in Iraq threatened Kuwait, fought the Kurds, and quarrelled with Iran; they also made some attempt to encourage nationalist forces elsewhere in the Gulf. But the agreement between Iran and Iraq in March 1975 seems to have ended this period: Iraq is now being re-integrated into the Gulf system, its major disputes are settled, or at least shelved, and its own government appears politically and economically more secure. Iraq's continuing opposition to Iranian and western policies is confined to the diplomatic context. The North Yemeni coup of 1962 represented a more serious threat to the emergence of a new order, since it released popular movements in territories under British rule. Although a conservative solution to the North Yemeni civil war was found in 1970, after eight years of conflict, the 1962 coup led to the outbreak of guerrilla war in Aden which, after four years of struggle, enabled the NLF to establish a People's Republic. Moreover after the start of guerrilla war in South Yemen in 1963, a guerrilla movement also began in Dhofar. By 1967, when Britain was scheduled to leave South Yemen, there was no alternative to accepting the NLF as the government there; but for several years after independence, South Yemeni exiles and other forces, supported by Saudi Arabia, tried to attack across the Republic's borders and undermine the regime. Now South Yemen has been, at least temporarily, accepted. In March 1976, Saudi Arabia even agreed to extend diplomatic recognition. As with Cuba, years of isolation failed to topple the government there. In Oman however, the counter-revolutionary forces have tried with more determination and success to eliminate the revolutionary movement, to stem the tide of popular opposition at the South Yemeni borders; the movement has been weaker than in South Yemen and Oman borders the oil producing areas. It has therefore been more possible *and* more necessary to crush the guerrillas there.

3. Saudi Iranian Condominium:

As Britain withdrew from the region in the 1960s, Saudi Arabia and Iran became the two dominant powers in the region. In US parlance, this is the 'twin pillar' policy. The dominant military role has fallen to Iran: it has a far larger population and army, whilst the main financial role has fallen to Saudi Arabia, whose influence spreads into many parts of the Arab world.[5] Iranian troops have fought in Oman, Iraq, Kurdistan and the Baluchistan area of Pakistan; Iranian advisers have served in North Yemen; Iranian Phantom jets were sent to South Vietnam in 1972; and Iranian naval vessels have begun to patrol the Indian Ocean in co-operation with South Africa. Saudi Arabia on the other hand has financed the royalist forces in the North Yemeni civil war, is aiding the denationalisation of the economies in Egypt and the Sudan, and has provided funds for the Sultan of Oman since 1971. Beyond the partnership of these two powers lies the prospect of a comprehensive Gulf security agreement involving the larger and smaller states but possibly including Iraq. Such a system, which has been under discussion since 1974 could be formal or informal, but in effect it would reproduce the Baghdad Pact in a post-colonial era, and ensure an integrated and stable repressive system in the whole region. As such it forms part of a wider shift to the right in the Arab world of which the central component has been Egypt's alliance with the USA, a shift which everywhere marks the end of the nationalist wave that began in the 1950s.

4. Economic and Social Modernisation:

Despite the production of oil for some decades, the societies of the Gulf and the Peninsula had hardly been affected at all by economic development until the mid-1950s. In the last two decades there has been a process of accelerated and interconnected change: increasing oil revenues, virtual nationalisation of the oil industry, expansion of civilian and military state structures, construction of infrastructures and welfare services. The availability of the oil revenues makes these changes possible; the need to preserve the existing regimes makes them essential. There have been considerable problems in this domain: in nearly all states sections of the ruling class have opposed the changes (Iranian landowners, Saudi traditionalists), and at times there have been acrimonious quarrels between the producer states and the oil companies over pricing and supply, quarrels that in 1973-74 led to threats on the part of the USA to invade the region. Nevertheless the overall record so far has been one of relatively harmonious and successful transformation of these states, a process that is still in its early stages.

Internationalisation in Oman

Of all the states in the region, Oman was the least affected by these policies until the British ousted reigning Sultan Said bin Taimur in 1970 and installed his son Qabus. Till then Britain retained sole economic, political and military control. The state was weak, indeed ramshackle: there were only 3 primary schools and in Dhofar the army had lost all of the populated area except the capital, Salala, to the guerrillas. There had been no economic development of any kind, except for limited oil production which began in 1967. Then, in response to the guerrilla threat and to the anomalous isolation of Oman, the country was belatedly introduced into the new order. Foreign companies moved in: Japanese, US, German, Swedish as well as British.[6] The state machine was expanded and staffed with expatriates or English-speaking Arabs from East Africa where local personnel were wanting. Roads, schools, hospitals, newspapers, television were introduced. And most importantly of all the armed forces were expanded. The army, The Sultan's Armed Forces, were expanded from around 3,000 to over 12,000. The Sultan of Oman's Air Force (SOAF) and the Sultan of Oman's Navy (SON) were likewise developed and acquired new equipment.

Yet this expansion of the Omani military apparatus is in some ways misleading. Within the Sultan's forces, foreign personnel play an important role. Up to half of the soldiers in the SAF are mercenaries from the impoverished plateau of Baluchistan, in Pakistan. All the top personnel, officers and training staff, in the three branches are British, and 'Omanisation' has so far gone very slowly. More importantly, there have been definite limits to the expansion of the 'Sultan's' forces which have only been supplemented by the introduction of other military forces. In 1975 at least nine foreign states had military personnel in Oman. Britain had over 1,500 men: about 700 were running the two RAF bases at Salala and Masirah; another 300 were mercenaries formerly in the British Army, commanded by serving British officers; the rest were either seconded British personnel, including the commanders of the so-called British Army Training Team, a force drawn from the counter-insurgency regiment of the Special Air Services, and used both for training Omani troops and for behind-the-lines missions. Although Britain handed over its two bases in March 1977, several hundred contract and seconded personnel remain.

The two other states with considerable contingents in Oman have been Jordan and Iran. Jordan has deployed several thousand troops there and also provided experts for the police and intelligence services: the first of these came in 1972-73 and the ground troops were deployed from February to September 1975. Iran began sending forces in 1972 when 30 helicopters and their crews were provided; but the main body, an estimated 4,000 troops, came in December 1973 and remained till most were withdrawn in early 1977. In addition to these three states two neighbouring Arab countries, the United Arab Emirates and Saudi Arabia have provided garrisons which have released SAF forces to fight at the front. Both Saudi Arabia and the Emirates have also provided financial aid. And it is a striking indication of Saudi Arabia's military weakness that, it, Oman's giant neighbour, cannot provide the forces to crush a movement in Dhofar which it opposes.[7] Further training activities have been carried out by officers from Pakistan, as well as by smaller groups from India and the Sudan. Their officers probably knew English and have worked on British equipment. Finally, in 1975, the USA sent a small training team to instruct the SAF in the use of TOW anti-tank missiles.

This internationalisation reflected two things: the weakness of the Omani and British positions, and a deliberate integration of Oman into the Gulf's new order. As we have seen not only has Oman been incapable of providing the officers and commanders required but it has even had to draw many of its rank-and-file from Baluchistan. Britain too was unable to meet the added requirements of the war, even if it had wanted to, since it is militarily overextended; with upwards of 15,000 troops in Northern Ireland since 1971, it has already been unable to meet its full commitment to NATO forces in Germany and could not have spared the forces for an Omani campaign. In addition, the commitment of large numbers of ground troops could have aroused political opposition at home. To fulfill the requirements of the Oman campaign, troops have been drawn from the two regional states capable of providing them — Jordan and Iran. These armies have been trained for some decades on western equipment; politically the countries are repressive monarchies, where no opposition to the involvement in Oman is likely to emerge. The political front inside aggressor states, so important in offsetting military disadvantages on the field of battle, has therefore been closed to the guerrillas. But the intervention of other powers served their specific interests too. Both Iran and Jordan have a strategic interest in sustaining a fellow conservative monarch, whilst the Shah has benefitted from the opportunity to train his forces in anti-guerrilla actions, and made a point of rotating them every 4 months to maximise experience.

This internationalisation is significant in a broader historical perspective. During the century of imperial domination (from the mid-nineteenth Century to 1945) each power tended to deal on its own with enemies within its sphere of influence. An exception to this was the expedition by a coalition of imperial powers against the Chinese nationalist forces, the so-called 'Boxers', in 1900.[8] But this was in a territory over which no specific states claimed jurisdiction. Another exception occurred after the Russian Revolution in 1917 when a joint counter-revolutionary intervention was mounted to try to crush the new regime. It was after World War II that co-operation increased substantially: Britain intervened in former Dutch and French colonies in the Far East (Vietnam, Indonesia) to restore their weaker colleagues (1945), whilst the USA encouraged the establishment of a number of regional alliances — NATO, SEATO, the Baghdad Pact.

Even the latter tended to be primarily designed to confront the Soviet Union and China; in their colonies, the respective powers — British, French, Dutch, Belgian, Portuguese — continued to handle their own affairs, as the USA did in Latin America. A new development was the Korean War (1950-54). The USA had occupied this former Japanese colony in 1945 and, using its control of the UN, had mobilised an international force when war broke out in 1950. No less than 15 other states fought with the USA and the South Korean forces. But this internationalisation was a political rather than a military one: in 1953, when there were 350,000 US troops in Korea, there were only 44,000 from the other states combined.[9] In Vietnam a similar political internationalisation occured: the main fighting was done by South Vietnamese and US troops, with much smaller contingents from South Korea, the Philippines and Thailand, and some support from Britain, Australia, New Zealand, Taiwan and Iran.

In one sense, Korea and Vietnam were transitional cases. Old-style internationalisation consisted of a group of states uniting against a specific enemy, as the European powers had done against Napoleon, and the imperial powers had against the Boxers and the Bolsheviks. New-style internationalisation involves an alliance between former imperial powers and new, militarily capable, regional powers. In Korea and Vietnam, elements of the new internationalisation can be seen, but in reality most of the fighting was done by the USA and its own local ally within the country concerned. The new internationalisation is much clearer in four other cases: Sri Lanka, Angola, Zaire and Oman. In April 1971 an underground movement backed mainly by peasant youth, the Janatha Vimukhti Peramuna staged an armed insurrection against the Bandaranaike government.[10] The movement was crushed within six weeks, but not before a number of foreign states had sent in military aid to back up the Sri Lanka armed forces: Britain and the USA did so; so too did India, Pakistan and Yugoslavia. While no forces from these countries fought on the ground, their aid was a substantial boost to the beleaguered government and illustrated a new pattern of military co-operation. In Angola an attempt was made, using Zaire and South Africa, as well as mercenaries, to defeat the revolution, whilst in Zaire in the spring of 1977 it was France and Morocco, with aid from the USA, Egypt, Sudan and Iran, that helped Mobutu to quell the rising in Shaba province.

In Oman, we can see the new internationalisation in its clearest form, with forces from an old imperial power supporting two regional powers fighting on the ground; here the old imperial power played a less active role on the front line than its two partners. Moreover, not only did Iran provide troops, but it also assumed responsibility for the air defence of Oman, stationing missiles and Phantom jets near the border with South Yemen. And this Iranian role provides the clue to deciphering one of the more hidden aspects of the war, the role of the USA. Formally, the only US involvement was miniscule — the provision of some TOW anti-tank missiles and of a small, temporary, training team.[11] A few US counter-insurgency experts probably worked with the Iranian force, but they did not play a major role. But since 1971 the CIA had been providing financial aid through Saudi Arabia to Oman, and provided electronic surveillance of the Omani coast under the cover of civilian American fishing ships. The most substantial US contribution, however, came through the Iranian force, since the USA provides most of the equipment and service facilities for the Iranians. Over one thousand US technicians are employed in Iran under contract to the Iranian army and air force. Whilst most are probably located in Oman itself the specific location is, in any case, trivial: it matters little whether a broken-down or damaged US helicopter gunship is repaired on the strip at Salala by a US technician, or whether the gunship is taken back to Iran for the same purpose.

Both the US and Britain played a vital role in the Oman war, but one that was not concentrated on the battle-field itself. The British SAS troops that fought on the front line in 1971 did so as irregular forces and in secret: there will no doubt be a role in the future for such small, highly mobile forces from the ex-imperial nations in counter-insurgency operations (the SAS could return to Malaya), while the main combat role will generally fall to the regional armies. This is the essence of the Nixon doctrine. Here Oman bears comparison with other such operations: in Timor, where it was the Indonesian armed forces that attacked FRETILIN; in Angola, where it was Zaire and South Africa which sent troops and passed on CIA money to the anti-MPLA forces; in Latin America, where Brazil, although not getting massively involved, has intervened in Bolivia, Chile, Uruguay and Argentina to support counter-revolutionary forces. No US troops have been landed in Latin America since the invasion of the Dominican Republic in 1965; yet US-trained forces have crushed guerrilla movements and assisted coups, a process in which Brazil has played the leading role.[12]

British Counter-Insurgency

This internationalisation of the Oman war, and the

delegation of roles to regional powers with the support of Britain and the USA has been superimposed on a conflict similar to others fought by the British army for a century and to which the lessons of this long experience have been applied. Indeed of all the colonial powers' the British experience in counter-insurgency is probably the richest. The Dutch (in Indonesia), the French (in Algeria) and the Portuguese (in southern Africa) all carried out counter-insurgency operations in their colonies. During World War II, Hitler's Wehrmacht carried out counter-partisan campaigns in Eastern Europe (especially in Russia and Yugoslavia). And the USA's actions in the Philippines (after 1896) and in Haiti (1916-1934) gave the US repressive apparatus a foretaste of its later operations. The British experience was gained in establishing, retaining and then terminating an Empire; it falls into three main phases: the century between the accession of Queen Victoria and the outbreak of World War II (1837-1939); the Second World War itself (1935-1945); and the three decades of counter-insurgency warfare since then (1945-1975).

In each of these periods the British army acquired an experience that helped it to face subsequent threats, even though these threats did not necessarily come from the same kind of enemy: there is a world of political difference between the South Arabian guerrillas of today and the Pathans of the North-West Frontier in the 19th Century. In the period of Queen Victoria's rule (to 1901) the British fought over 45 small colonial wars: characteristic of the period were the campaigns in India against the nationalist uprising of 1857, in the Sudan against the Mahdi, in South

Africa against the Zulus, and later the Boers, in the Middle East against the Egyptians, and in the Far East against the people of China. In this century of colonial rule, up to 1939 they had acquired a number of skills later put to good use: in India and Africa they developed the techniques of constructing native armies using British officers; in the Boer war they developed the system of population control — 20,000 Boers died of disease in concentration camps, after the British Army had divided the countryside with barbed wire and built over 8,000 block houses. In the 1920s, in Iraq, Somalia and South Yemen, the RAF pioneered the use of airpower against colonial enemies, as a mechanism of control far more economical than the use of ground troops.

The second phase of British counter-insurgency experience, World War II, was mainly a war against a conventional enemy, but it provided lessons that were extremely useful in postwar campaigns, as well as supplying the personnel for such activities. In the war against Japan in South-East Asia, the British developed techniques of jungle warfare which were later codified and taught at a Jungle Warfare School at Kota Tingi in Malaya, an establishment at which US, Thai, Philippine and other troops were trained during the Vietnam War.[13] Another World War II development was the setting up of the Special Air Services Regiment, a unit of volunteers used originally for operations behind German lines in the North African desert and subsequently re-organised for counter-insurgency operations.[14] Finally, the postwar campaigns borrowed heavily on the experiences of the British Army in psychological warfare against the

German occupation forces in Europe.

In the postwar period, Britain has lost its Empire, but it has also fought over thirty medium and small-scale military operations to crush forces it did not want to hand over power to, or to dictate the terms on which it did hand over power. It has faced the problem that the forces it was fighting in the colonies, while militarily weak, have been politically on the ascendant; added to this is the problem that Britain's military posture has been directed against a conventional enemy — Russia. The latter problem has been solved by the fact that no war with Russia actually occurred and the three conventional campaigns Britain has fought have been against colonial foes: Korea (1950-1954), Suez (1956), and Kuwait (1961).

Leaving aside these three conventional operations and some subversive operations there have been over 30 medium and small operations in the colonial arena during the post-war period.[15] Of these 10 were of significant dimensions — i.e. they involved several thousand troops, over a number of years, in sizeable military operations. These ten were:

1. *Greece, 1944-1947:*

This was a war to restore the Greek monarchy and to crush the communist guerrillas who controlled most of the country in 1944. British troops launched the first counter-offensive in 1944-45 and Britain supported the Greek Royalists until the USA took over main responsibility in 1947 (the Truman doctrine).

2. *Palestine, 1946-1948:*

This was a campaign by the British Army against the underground Jewish forces fighting to establish an

Israeli state. Britain pulled out in 1948, leaving the field open for the first Arab-Israeli war.

3. *Malaya, 1948-1960:*
This was the most protracted and important postwar operation: the military campaign of the Malayan Communist party was defeated although it has now revived again in the mid-1970s.

4. *Kenya, 1953-1956:*
The campaign of the Land Freedom Army (known abusively by the British as 'Mau Mau') was militarily crushed, but in 1960 Kenya became independent under Jomo Kenyatta, the leader of that campaign.

5. *Cyprus, 1955-1959:*
Here the military campaign of EOKA was contained, if not defeated, but the British government in the end handed power over to the forces led by Archbishop Makarios.

6. *Oman, 1957-59:*
This was a campaign to crush a nationalist uprising by the tribes of the interior of Northern Oman, who were then backed by Egypt, Russia and China and to some extent by Saudi Arabia and the USA as well. The movement was destroyed militarily in early 1959.

7. *South Yemen, 1963-1967:*
Beginning as a guerrilla war in the mountains north of Aden, this campaign spread to the town of Aden itself in 1964 and in the end Britain withdrew and handed power to the National Liberation Front.

8. *Borneo, 1961-1965:*
This was a campaign along the border between

Malaysia and Indonesia on the island of Borneo, in which the guerrillas received the support of Indonesian President Sukarno. His policy of 'confrontation' ended with the coup which overthrew his regime in September 1965.

9. *Oman II, 1965-1976.*

10. *Northern Ireland, 1969 onwards:*

What began as an operation to keep feuding Catholic and Protestant communities apart, has since 1972 become the world's most developed urban guerrilla conflict, with the British Army facing attack from both Catholic and Protestant groups and the two communities attacking each other. Despite the different political character, many of the technical-military aspects are similar to those in other counter-insurgency campaigns.

The conditions under which these campaigns were fought were predominantly rural, varying from jungle (Malaya, Kenya, Borneo, Oman II) to more arid and desert conditions (Oman I, the South Yemeni mountains). Some of the rural campaigns had an urban component (Kenya, South Yemen) whilst two have been predominantly urban counter-insurgency campaigns (Cyprus, Northern Ireland). The rural ones bore most resemblance to the classic colonial campaigns of the imperial epoch. However, the most striking feature of the eight campaigns that are now over is that the British Army has been relatively successful in its operations. In five campaigns the enemy were militarily and politically defeated: Greece, Malaya, Oman I, Borneo, Oman II. In two others the guerrillas were either militarily almost crushed (Kenya) or contained (Cyprus) before a political agreement between them and Britain was reached.

The political balance sheet is even more favourable: in addition to the four outright victories, Kenya and Cyprus were in the end politically favourable to Britain, and the independent states allowed British troops to retain facilities in their countries. In Palestine too the British had little cause for political concern: eight years after the forces who fought Britain had established the state of Israel, the latter's army had joined with France and Britain in a military campaign against Nasser's Egypt. Only in South Yemen did a guerrilla movement challenge the terms of British decolonisation and win against determined British opposition, after which it continued to support the guerrilla movement in the neighbouring state of Oman.

The British Army also gained — and in the case of Ireland continues to gain — a rich experience in counter-insurgency activity from this post-war series of campaigns. Drawing on the experience of World War II they further developed such specialities as jungle warfare and psychological war: the latter, using 'misinformation' against the enemy has involved a skilled manipulation of the press. A further development has been the use of psychological torture: this has involved the development of special disorientation techniques against which heroic but unsuspecting militants have had no recourse. The incidence of this goes back to the Malayan campaign, but was only exposed properly twenty years later in Northern Ireland. It is therefore not for nothing that throughout the postwar period representatives of foreign armies have continually come to Britain to seek advice on how to conduct their own counter-insurgency campaigns.

The Omani Experience

The accumulated legacy of British counter-insurgency has therefore been drawn from a wide variety of experience and has produced a body of lessons that has been available not only to the British Army but also to the armies of Britain's allies (the USA in Vietnam, the Portuguese in Africa) and to the new regional powers.[16] Three of the ten significant post-war campaigns have been fought in South Arabia: one in South Yemen and the other two in Oman.

The first Omani war (1957-1959) took place in the barren mountains of northern Oman, and ended when British SAS troops stormed the guerrilla stronghold on the main mountain plateau of the interior in January 1959. This earlier campaign demonstrated that the position of the Sultan was militarily very weak: his army of around 2,500 relied on British officers and Baluchi mercenaries. The so-called Sultan of Oman's Air Force was a hastily assembled force, created by the British in 1958 and relying entirely on British pilots and servicing personnel. The British were able to crush the rebellion because the latter was poorly organised and armed and because its bases were easily surrounded; air attacks on villages and irrigation channels, combined with the introduction of SAS forces from Malaya finally overcame resistance. Indeed it was the success of SAS units in Oman that formed the basis of Britain's defence policy in the early 1960s, in which mobile units of British troops were to be held ready to intervene east of Suez where need so dictated.[17]

The second Omani war has taken place in quite different social and geographical conditions in the southern province of Dhofar. Although at first led by a traditional tribal leadership, the guerilla movement was in 1968 transformed into a self-proclaimed revolutionary People's Front which sought to liberate the whole Gulf and to carry through a social revolution in the area it had freed. By 1970 the guerrillas had conquered nearly the whole of the inhabited mountainous part of Dhofar (two-thirds of the province is desert), and were able to shell the RAF installations in the Dhofari capital, Salala. It was only in July 1970 that the British deposed the reigning Sultan, installed his son Qabus who had been trained at British military establishments, and began a counter-offensive which with Iranian and Jordanian help had reconquered much of Dhofar by the end of 1975.

The course of this war reflects the advantages and disadvantages enjoyed by each side. The geography of the Dhofar region gave the guerrillas some advantages in their campaign. The operative military area is about 200 miles long and 20-50 miles deep, a block of tropical hills between the desert and the sea which from June to September enjoys monsoon rains. Here the People's Front enjoyed two advantages: first there are good on-the-ground conditions, with very rough country, virtually no roads, relatively thick vegetation and a mass of limestone caves enabling them to store supplies, hide and shelter with ease; secondly, at its south-west end Dhofar borders on South Yemen, which since independence in 1967 has supported the guerrillas with arms, food and facilities. But against these guerrilla advantages must be set the greater geographical advantages enjoyed by the counter-insurgency forces.

First the total area to be controlled is very small — less than 10,000 square miles — and hence presents far smaller problems of subjugation than most recent counter-insurgency campaigns (South Vietnam for example is over sixty times larger). The population is at most 100,000. Secondly the guerrilla area is extremely exposed, particularly near the South Yemeni border where the tropical cover is less than four miles across between the desert and the sea. Moreover, not only were the Sultan's forces able to bombard the liberated areas from the sea and from the air, but they could also do so from the desert; here they enjoyed a complete advantage, since the desert, being rather flat and without cover, is unusable by guerrillas. A contrast with Vietnam presents itself here: in Vietnam the guerrillas were exposed from the sea and the US fleet made the most of it, but the NLF were covered on their western flank by Laos and this offered them protection and a number of different supply routes. In Dhofar on the other hand, the counter-insurgency forces controlled both sides of the combat zone; it is as if the NLF supplies in South Vietnam had had to be brought in over the 17th parallel border and through the DMZ, while the US and allied forces could have attacked from secure bases in Laos, in addition to using their naval and coastal advantages.

A further advantage enjoyed by the counter-insurgency forces was the fact that their base areas remained secure. Despite successive attempts in 1970, 1972 and 1974 the People's Front failed to expand its military activities out of Dhofar and, across 500 miles of desert, into northern Oman. Indeed this desert barrier and the PFLO's weakness in northern Oman were the most important overall limitations to the expansion of the guerrilla movement. In Dhofar itself, the government headquarters at Salala was impregnable since it is backed by sea, from which government reinforcements can always be brought in; and is separated from the mountains by a 10 mile radius of flat territory across which the guerrillas, armed only with light weapons, were never able to advance. Although from 1968 to 1973 the guerrillas were able to shell the airfield at Salala and in 1972, they held Mirbat, a coastal town near Salala, for some hours, their operations were in general confined to the mountain regions.

Nor are the social conditions in the area very favourable to the guerrillas. There has existed a long tradition of tribal unrest in Dhofar, which has been directed against the Omani Sultans, who occupied the area and overtaxed it. Once Dhofari men began to work in the oil states in the 1950s, a nationalist opposition based on these migrant workers began to emerge. But Dhofari society itself retains its predominantly tribal character and especially in the east, the most densely populated part of the region, the guerrilla movement encountered considerable traditionalist opposition. Tribal leaders were prepared to work with the People's Front during the easier phase of struggle (1965-1970); but once the military conditions became harsher and once the Sultan was able to offer material attractions to the tribes, it became evident that the counter-insurgency campaign had a potential social base in Dhofar, both amongst tribal groups that had been neutral and amongst those that no longer backed the Front.

Another dimension in which the Sultan has had an advantage is in the resources at his command. Oil has been produced in Oman since 1967, and the quadrupling of oil prices in 1973, although in no way a result of the Sultan's actions, has brought increased income to the Omani state. In 1974 revenue was £600 millions; consequently the Sultan had the money to purchase the arms and personnel he needed in order to continue the military campaign in Dhofar and to pursue a *hearts and minds* campaign designed to win, or at least confuse, the population (see below).

The People's Front for the Liberation of Oman, by contrast, was able to carry out a development programme in the areas under its control, but it was hampered both by the lack of financial resources and, later, by the bombardment to which the liberated areas were subjected. The first schools, medical centres and agricultural developments in Dhofar were all set up by the Front; but since 1970, when the Omani government development programme got under way, the material advantages were increasingly on the side of the counter-insurgency forces.

The PFLO was also militarily weak and guerrilla weaponry has remained poor: until 1975 the Front had only a few anti-aircraft guns, some mortars and light artillery plus its AK-47 Kalashnikov rifles. The Front had no reply to the long-range naval and artillery bombardment of the enemy and only in the autumn of 1975 did they acquire the SAM-7 missiles required to counter British and Iranian air power.

Counter-Insurgency Tactics in Dhofar

In the first five years, up to 1970, the British were on the defensive and merely tried to hold out with their ramshackle army and colonial administration. The main tactics used were traditional ones: villages were burnt to punish the populations, corpses of guerrilla fighters were hung up to rot in the main square of Salala; the mountains were blockaded and Salala itself was ringed with a barbed wire fence so that no food could be taken out or weapons brought in. However, by 1968 the evident and dangerous failure of these policies, and the incompetence of the ruling Sultan who had been in power since 1932, led the British to plan alternative measures. The 1970 coup took place as a result.

The first major counter-offensive occurred in October-November 1971, when the government established new positions in the eastern Dhofari mountains after a combined force of British and Omani troops had attacked from the desert. In 1972 a similar operation took place in Western Dhofar and an outpost was built on a 4,000 feet high hill at Sarfeet near the Yemeni border. In 1973, a 35-mile barrier, the Hornbeam Line, was built between the desert and the sea some miles west of Salala, and in December of that year Iranian forces opened a road running from Salala through the mountains to the desert. In November-December 1974, the Iranians attacked in Western Dhofar, and by the spring of 1975 they had set up a second barrier, the Demavand line, about 15 miles from the South Yemeni Border; so guerrilla units remaining east of the Demavand and Hornbeam lines have been deprived of supplies and have been easier to attack. In late 1975 the Iranians and SAF were able to build a third line along the border which effectively excluded PFLO forces from Dhofar.

Three specific military factors that have been effective in Dhofar are air power, long-range bombardment and the construction of the communications barriers just mentioned. Until 1972-73 the SOAF used its jets and turbo-prop planes for reconnaissance and for bombarding suspect guerrilla supply lines: the introduction of helicopters by Iran and by SOAF itself (in 1972-73) then enabled the counter-insurgency campaign to establish fortified positions in the mountains such as the one in Sarfeet, which could be supplied only by air. But in the absence of any qualified troops, helicopters cannot be used for heliborne troop attacks, and the first time Omani ground forces were involved in such an operation was in February 1975 against People's Front forces north-west of Salala, in the Mammarr region.

Throughout the 1970-75 period, however, air power was used to bomb the liberated areas and to disrupt the life of the fighters and the civilian inhabitants there. It formed part of a broader policy of long-range bombardment which had not till then been seen in British counter-insurgency operations, although it was familiar from US policy in Vietnam, and was later used by the Indonesians in Timor. Planes, ships and long-range artillery have all been used in this way, usually as a preliminary to an attack by ground troops. In October 1975, the Iranian Navy fired 1,500 shells into a six-mile stretch of territory between the coastal villages of Dhalqut and Rakhyut as a preliminary to occupation by Iranian and SAF forces. The purpose of this was to eliminate guerrilla forces and to coerce the population into seeking shelter in government-held areas.

The third practice mentioned, communications barriers, was designed to prevent the Front from sending arms and food to its units further inside Dhofar. Mountain positions like Sarfeet, overlooking PFLO supply lines impeded guerrilla communications and drew off guerrilla forces and ammunition that would otherwise have been used elsewhere; but despite the narrowness of the distance between Sarfeet and the sea (less than four miles) the guerrillas were until late 1975 able to move their supplies through on camels and donkeys. Their lines to central Dhofar were only stopped by the creation of the Hornbeam and Demavand lines which had unattended ground sensors at specific points and platoons of troops at regular intervals. From then on guerrilla supplies had to be carried through by human beings. These barriers also represent a development in British counter-insurgency practice; although the French had built a line over 300 miles long between Tunisia and Algeria during the Algerian war, and unattended sensors had been developed (without much success) by the US forces in Indo-China, the British had not used this tactic effectively in the past. For reasons that are unclear, they have not yet tried to erect such a barrier along the 270-mile frontier between Ulster and the Irish republic.

At the organisational and political levels of the Dhofar counter-insurgency, the legacy of the previous periods is clear. As elsewhere the SAS played a special and concealed role. They participated in the

October-November 1971 campaign in Eastern Dhofar, the only time it is certain that British infantry were used in front-line engagements, and after that they formed a British Army Training Team which trained Dhofari irregulars, the *firqas,* and fought with these irregulars in mountain operations. They also work with their combat role and the British government denies that the SAS participated in offensive actions, admitting only that they *'seek out realistic training situations'* and *'if fired upon, they will fire back'*. Another familiar presence in British counter-insurgency operations were the Gurkhas: these mercenaries from the Nepalese Himalaya have also been in Dhofar, and in 1974 some were decorated for bravery as a result.

The Dhofari *firqas* are counter-guerrilla units modelled on the *'counter-gangs'* of Kenya: as in Kenya they are recruited from deserters from the guerrilla forces. There are estimated to be about 2,000 Dhofaris organised in this way, most of them tribesmen who have deserted from the Front since 1970. The *firqas* play a more important role, however, than the *'counter-gangs'* of Kenya, since the latter were mainly restricted to intelligence-gathering, while the *firqas* have been used for raiding the liberated areas, and, most ominously, for holding down reconquered territories. It is this latter policy that presents the greatest threat for the future of Dhofar and which is reversing the Front's attempts to eliminate tribal differences in the mountains.

Before the beginnings of the revolutionary movement the basis of inter-tribal feuding was conflict over water wells; one of the first steps taken by the Front in its attempt to eliminate tribalism was to declare all water the common property of the people, and not the property of a specific tribe. What is now happening in the Dhofari mountains is that specific *firqas,* each of which is organised on a tribal basis, are reclaiming control of water sources and restricting the access of other tribes. The comment of one pro-British writer is clear on this:

> 'It is the government's policy in siting water wells to encourage a tribal intermingling. The existence of the *firqas* directly contradicts that policy. Well armed and regularly paid, some of them are in a position to run a highly efficient protection racket based on access to water' [18]

Population control and food control were also integral parts of the counter-insurgency campaign in Dhofar. The paradigm for this is the Malayan campaign where in 1951-1953 over half a million Malayan Chinese were resettled in around 600 new villages in order to break their contact with the guerrilla movement. In Kenya, over 1 million people were forcibly resettled during the counter-insurgency campaign (see also note 16). These tactics have a double function: to deprive the guerrillas of supplies and support and to coerce the civilian population into accepting government control. While the resettlement policy has been less widespread than in Malaya, nine centres have been established in the mountains in order to enable the government to carry this policy through. After the simple food control measures of the late 1960s (enforced around Salala), this new policy was developed with on the one hand the construction of settlements run by *firqas* and on the other, a systematic attack on those areas outside government control designed to push the population into these centres and into government-held areas. Wells have been attacked, fields burnt, camels, cattle and goats strafed from the air. The population who remain outside government control were therefore subjected not only to bombardment, but also to the danger of starvation: by 1973 malnutrition and diseases resulting from it such as trachoma had increased in the liberated areas. The largest regrouping centre of all was in the environs of Salala: those who did not stay in the mountain resettlement centres were housed in new cheap units built on the Salala plain, where they were given a salary and kept under careful surveillance. In writing on Malaya, Sir Robert Thompson, head of the British Advisory Mission in Vietnam from 1961 to 1965, has written:

> 'The fundamental aim behind the establishment of the security framework based on strategic hamlets is to isolate the insurgent both physically and politically from the population'.[19]

This describes well the population control measures used in Dhofar. Control even went to the extent of branding the cattle of the mountain people so that a check can be kept on whether they are being moved about or used by the People's Front guerrillas.

Integral to this attack on the population was the psychological warfare campaign being conducted by the government. Leaflet drops, radio, loudspeaker broadcasts from government positions, and, since 1974, colour TV have all been used to reach the fighters and the population in the liberated areas or, in the case of TV, to reinforce government control of those in the reconquered zone. One of the main purposes of the campaign was, as in Malaya, to encourage members of the guerrilla forces to surrender, and this was done by a mixture of carrot and stick methods.

The most obvious carrot was money: the equivalent of £50 was offered for information on arms caches. Security from bombardment was another inducement. The regime also went so far as to criticise the People' Front for emancipating women and limiting to one the number of wives a man can have; those men who cross over to the government side were allowed to have four again, as is traditional in Muslim societies. The stick side of the surrender campaign was terror: a leaflet dropped over western Dhofar in 1973, for example, proclaimed that *'Military planes, cannons and automatic weapons are out hunting for you. Wherever you have crept, they will teach you a lesson and in the end will kill you all'*. Those who run such psychological war campaigns are well aware that leaflets of this kind are most effective *after* a preliminary softening up process, after, for example, guerrilla food supplies have begun to run short and the guerrilla area has been subjected to systematic bombardment.

British writers discussing Malaya have in particular stressed the use of guerrillas who cross over to the government side, what in counter-insurgency jargon are called SEPs (Surrendered Enemy Personnel). In Malaya, SEPs were used for intelligence, for propaganda films and for undercover operations; in Dhofar, many of those who crossed over did so in 1970, so their information became outdated, but the individual desertions that continued provided the government with a basis for one leaflet campaign: sheets of paper with the picture and details of an SEP were dropped over the liberated areas, and the text related how so-and-so was duped by the communists, then, revolted by their practices he decided to rally to the cause of Islam and loyalty to Sultan Qabus. Such leaflets may have little effect on politically formed cadres, but they do strike home at the less politically-conscious members of the guerrilla force, and PFLO lost a considerable number of fighters through desertion. Whereas in the early days (1970-72) many of the leaflets failed because they were apparently written in bad Arabic by British intelligence officers, they had more effect when Jordanian intelligence personnel were brought in to provide technical assistance in the campaign.

Parallel to this campaign, the government tried to split the population from the guerrilla force. Large rewards were being offered for the half dozen men considered by the British as being the most important members of the Front: when I was in western Dhofar in 1973 I remember well the amazement on the face of one man who had just deserted to the guerrillas from the Sultan's Army, and found he was eating next to the notorious Said Dublan for whose head he had been offered several thousand pounds only a week beforehand. Another tactic is indicated by the notebook of a British officer, Captain M. R. A. Campbell, who was killed by the Front in 1971: this contained details of how the Sultan's Army were laying mines with Russian markings near waterholes used by the civilian population in an attempt to discredit the guerrillas. But the main appeal of the Sultan was based on the three factors listed by Sir Robert Thompson in his study of Malaya — nationalism, religion and material wellbeing.

Despite the evident reliance of the Sultan on numerous foreign powers, an attempt was made to rally some sense of Arab Nationalism behind the regime. One of the *firqas* is known as the *Gamal Abd-al Nasser firqat:* official statements by the regime rather preposterously compare 23 July 1952 when the Nationalist military coup took place in Egypt, to 23 July 1970 when Qabus replaced his father. In 1975, Muscat radio, run by Egyptian personnel, took to broadcasting Nasserist songs from the 1950s.

More plausible are religion and material wellbeing. Despite the fact that the Front has never criticised religion, the very fact that the guerrillas do not invoke Islam and attacked some of the institutions associated with Islam (e.g. polygamy), has enabled the Sultan to invoke Islam against the Front. In Dhofar the government has brought in two dozen religious instructors from the al-Azhar mosque in Cairo, and has made a point of repainting the mosque in villages it took over. How far this policy has served a purpose is hard to tell, and probably the greatest impact has been in Northern Oman, where religious feeling is stronger than in Dhofar.

As for material wellbeing, since 1970 the Sultan has opened schools, clinics and veterinary centres in Dhofar, while government propaganda has tried to portray the guerrillas as an essentially destructive force: government spokesmen allege, for example, that the guerrillas carried out no reforms in the mountain regions they controlled. The truth is that the *material* changes brought about by the government have been greater, while the *social and ideological* framework of Dhofari society (tribalist, authoritarian, religious) has remained the same in government-controlled areas.

The PFLO carried out fundamental social and ideological changes in the areas it liberated: in particular, it campaigned against the ideas and institutions that had sustained tribal conflict and the oppression of women. The Sultan has done nothing to alter these and has indeed reinforced them. But the Front's capacity for social change was limited by the meagre material resources at its disposal and by the increasingly destructive impact of the government's attack on the liberated areas. It was not able to build many schools or hospitals or roads, as the government could, and the changes in social relations were less visible amongst a population whose immediate concern has been survival in the face of air and artillery bombardment.

The International Dimension

These weaknesses on the ground were complemented by the extremely weak position of the PFLO on the external political front, outside Oman, in the rest of the Arab world, in Britain, in Europe and North America. There was no major diplomatic opposition to the British role in Oman. No other imperialist power opposed the British role, nor did any major Arab power, nor, after 1971, did the People's Republic of China. What a contrast this is with the situation during the first Oman War, when the conservative and tribal forces of the Imam received the noisy support of Egypt, Saudi Arabia, Russia, China and even the USA which at that time was challenging Britain's position in the region.

The only power that gave full support to the PFLO was South Yemen, an impoverished and beleaguered state that paid a high price for its solidarity. The Soviet Union also provided support after 1971. But most of the Arab world was disinterested. Libya gave financial aid and Qaddafi once threatened to send Libyan troops to Oman if the Iranians would not withdraw. Iraq provided some material and propaganda support on an intermittent basis up to 1975; but after the March 1975 agreement between Iraq and Iran, the Ba'thist government in Baghdad tempered its official support; later in the year it exchanged diplomatic relations with Sultan Qabus, while still publicising PFLO activities. Syria never lifted a finger to aid PFLO and was even less likely to do so after it built its alliance with King Hussein of Jordan. PFLO strongly criticised the Syrian intervention in Lebanon in 1976. Egypt, the former champion of Arab nationalism, expelled the PFLO office from Cairo in 1972 and in February 1976, Sadat paid an official visit to Muscat. In any case, Egypt has been a close collaborator of Saudi Arabia's since 1967. For its part, Algeria has recognised Qabus but allowed a small PFLO office to open in Algiers, and after the dispute over Western Sahara broke out in 1975, the Algerian media devoted some attention to the struggle in Oman. The whole Arab world proclaimed its support, at least in words, for the struggle of the people of Palestine. But in the second Palestine, in Oman, the nationalists and 'revolutionaries' have not been so willing to defend their principles. The Front was therefore prevented from mobilising the kind of international support enjoyed by the Algerians, the Palestinians and the Vietnamese.

The Front was further isolated by the kind of media control operated by the British. The assumptions and techniques of previous British campaigns were deployed and helped to prevent any serious protests from being made. During the counter-insurgency operation in the Radfan mountains of South Yemen (1963-64) the British government encountered some domestic opposition after press reports of a 'food control' campaign in which 50,000 South Yemenis had been driven out of their villages and had had their crops burnt. The High Commissioner at the time later commented that *'it was the publicity which did the damage'*,[20] in Dhofar no such mistake was made.

The British enjoyed three advantages in controlling the news about Oman. First of all, the level of British military involvement was numerically low even though the British force formed the backbone of the whole counter-insurgency operation: in 1975, there were about 1,500 military personnel (all volunteers) in Oman, of which less than a third were near the front line. Hence British casualties were very minimal — at most 10 or 20 a year. The kinds of domestic concern caused in France, Portugal or the USA over their colonial wars, did not pose a danger. The scale of the war, plus the fact that front-line actions were performed by Baluchi, Jordanian and Iranian troops (countries where, as has been said, no protests would be heard), enabled Britain to direct the war without shouldering the political burden of having to send quantities of men into the field.

A second and related advantage is the fact that the war cost Britain relatively little: the Sultan paid for the wages of the seconded British personnel (i.e. the money has been deducted from Omani oil revenues) and the traditional argument against colonial entanglements on economic grounds was hard to sustain. This was all the more so since British participation in the war had an obvious politico-economic payoff — viz. the goodwill of the rulers of the Gulf, and in particular of Saudi Arabia and Iran, whose financial backing was essential for the ailing British pound and for the British economy as a whole.

The most important advantage enjoyed by Britain in this respect was the simple fact that so little was heard about the Oman War, and most of what was heard was purveyed by journalists close to the official British position. Oman had no British settlers, no white missionaries, no independent or meddling observers who might be given credence in the rest of the world. No permanent correspondents covered the war. On the contrary, the press were only allowed in on supervised visits. Many of the events there were simply hushed up: the role of British troops in the 1971 autumn offensive only became known through an official leak some months later; similarly, it was two months before the Shah admitted that he had sent counter-insurgency forces into Oman in December 1973. No journalist covered the war till 1970 but then the policy of silence gave way to one of restriction and selected revelation.

A special information apparatus executed this policy. In London, a public relations firm, Michael Rice and Co., handled the Sultan's account, and in 1975 the Foreign Office seconded a significant official, a Mr. Tony Ashworth, to the Ministry of Information in

Muscat. Ashworth had previously worked in Aden and had been in charge of the Foreign Office's 'China-watching bureau in Hong Kong — the Regional Information Office. As an expert in psychological war and a senior intelligence officer, his job presumably included more than the mere distribution of government statements. The British government have been helped in this policy by the historically-generated disposition of British journalists to accept what they are told, not necassarily out of any dishonesty, but because they share the same ideological universe as their informants. The same tendency has been seen in Northern Ireland. Many journalists accepted, for example, that the British had not been behind the 1970 coup in Salala *('Whitehall seemed genuinely short of information . . . ')*. None questioned the tactics being used by the British to crush the resistance of the Dhofar population; none ever probed the corruption in the Sultan's administration — it was left to an American journalist, Jim Hoagland of the *Washington Post,* to start reporting this in 1975.

The complementary historical factor is that the stories put about by the British journalists fell on fertile ground; the official press liaison people put out those myths that are most likely to be accepted. Reports in 1970-71 made great play of alleged guerrilla brutalities, while in the same period it was on several occasions falsely claimed that Chinese officers had been seen fighting with the Front. Some non-British journalists, less prone to collude, have not been so welcome in Oman and have been treated less cordially; the French journalists Simonne and Jean Lacouture tell in their book of what happened when they visited Salala in late 1974. Whilst three British journalists were taken off on a helicopter by the RAF to visit government positions in the mountains (it crashed on take-off), the Lacoutures were greeted by an Omani official who offered to show them the province's development projects. When they asked about the war, he told them to enquire in Muscat, 500 miles away.[21]

At times a remarkable screening process seemed to operate in official publications. For example, an official British list of places where psychological torture has been practised (issued in 1972) names most incidents by country, but it then resorts to the phrase *'Persian Gulf 1970-71'* to disguise the country where this actually occurred, when there can be no doubt it was Oman.[22] Another case is to be found in Frank Kitson's *Low Intensity Operations* (1971), the most famous of all recent British counter-insurgency books and the one which provoked significant interest in Britain because it was held to be discussing the possibilities of a military takeover in the UK itself. In his discussion of psychological warfare Kitson discusses the deployment of 'PSYOPS' staff' (PSYOPS = psychological operations) in training establishments within Britain, and then goes on:

> 'So far as service manned teams are concerned, there is only one in existence which consists of an officer and eleven men. This is operating at the moment and is subsidized by the government of the territory in which it is deployed' (p. 188).

There can be little doubt about which country Kitson is referring to, nor why its name was withheld.

Conclusion

Oman was, in the words of one British officer *'the last place in the world where an Englishman is still called sahib'*, an almost anachronistic part of a long tradition of British colonial wars. But it also served as an indication of the continued relevance of much of this experience, and of how this kind of campaign can be combined with new forms of counter-insurgency (helicopters, electronic sensors), and with an internationalisation characteristic of the post-colonial world. In their attempt to win their freedom, the people of Oman have brought down on their heads an astounding force of repression.

Summarising the balance of forces, it is evident that:

1. *Militarily,*
the People's Front were fighting in a very restricted environment, with forces that were far too weak in numbers and firepower, against an enemy that had an overwhelming superiority in every respect.

2. *Politically,*
PFLO had some advantages in Dhofar, but these were more than offset by the character of some of its support there, and by its inability to open a second front in Northern Oman.

3. *Strategically,*
PFLO was almost without allies, facing an unprecedented coalition of determined and strong enemies, and was precluded for a number of reasons from mobilising strong international support.

Despite the existing situation, there is no reason to

assume that the present counter-revolutionary regime in Oman will survive, and indeed there are several factors suggesting the opposite. The country is ruled by an autocratic Sultan who is kept in power by thousands of foreign troops occupying Omani territory. These forces have been able to contain popular opposition for the time being but the military and economic oppression of the country is certain to produce continued nationalist hostility to the regime and may do so even inside the army.

Secondly, Oman is not a rich country, and despite claims by the Muscat authorities to the contrary, Oman's oil output will start falling in 1977 from its present peak. It may dry up around 1990. The resulting drop in government revenue will produce problems for the Sultan, and he has already been forced to cut development spending and to borrow from Saudi Arabia and Iran.

Furthermore, new problems are being created. The economic changes brought about since 1970 have been based mainly on disproportionate investment in the coastal region around Muscat: the interior of the country has been neglected, and much of the employment provided has been short-term, in the construction industry. The large shanty-towns growing around Muscat and the depopulation of the North Omani interior are indices of this process.

In Dhofar, the British are now concerned at the difficulties arising in the reconquered territories as a result of the gangster-like practices of their proteges, the *firqas*.

PFLO has certainly suffered severe military blows, but it has stated its determination to continue its struggle by all means at its disposal until its aims are met. Meanwhile, the underlying reasons for popular opposition to the Muscat regime certainly remain and are, in some ways, increasing.

FOOTNOTES
1. An earlier draft of this paper was prepared for inclusion in a reader on the Gulf projected by the Transnational Institute, Amsterdam.
2. There was no oil-production in Dhofar, and the Gulf's main fields are some hundreds of miles away. But had Dhofar, let alone the whole of Oman, fallen to the guerrillas, this would have threatened the political situation in the Gulf, as well as have opened the possibility of military conflicts involving producer states.
3. See, especially, on the military side, Michael Klare "Gunboat Diplomacy", and Eqbal Ahmad and David Caploe "The Logic of Military Intervention", in *Race and Class*, London, Winter 1976.
4. The main regional members of CENTO were Iran, Turkey and Pakistan, with Britain and the USA playing a backup role.
5. Iran's population is over 30 millions; Saudi Arabia's not more than 5 millions; Iran's armed forces total 250,000, Saudi Arabia's 50,000.
6. See *'Oil and Investment in Oman'*, the Gulf Committee, London, 1974.
7. Another reason for Saudi non-intervention may have been the long-standing hostility between the two monarchies over control of the Buraimi oasis in Northern Oman. But this could not have stood in the way of a Saudi desire to assert its power *and* keep out the Iranians, had it been able to do so.
8. Six foreign countries participated in the 1900 expedition against Peking: Britain, France, Germany, Russia, USA, Japan. Japan, the newest but nearest state, provided the main contingent and used its contribution to force concessions elsewhere from its senior partners (I am grateful to Walter Easey for this point).
9. The 15 other states were: Australia, Belgium, Canada, Columbia, Ethiopia, France, Greece, Luxemburg, Netherlands, New Zealand, Philippines, Thailand, Turkey, South Africa, and Britain. Most sent infantry battalions or brigades.
10. See Fred Halliday, "Armed insurrection in Ceylon", *New Left Review* 69.
11. The missiles were probably designed for use in a possible conflict with South Yemen, although Omani sources later claimed they had intended to use them against guerrillas who were holding out in caves.
12. See *NACLA Report* May-June 1975: *'Brazil, the continental strategy'*.

13. On the Jungle Warfare School, see the *Far Eastern Economic Review,* 11 September 1971. Britain also contributed to the US effort in Vietnam by sending a military advisory team, headed by a Malaya veteran, Sir Robert Thompson.
14. SAS are the British equivalent of the US Green Berets. They have special equipment, receive training in relevant languages, and are highly secretive.
15. For a list of British operations, see Julian Paget, *Counter-insurgency campaigning.* Apart from overt campaigns, the British state has also engaged in a number of undercover subversive operations against hostile governments. Two known campaigns of this kind are the ones against the People's Republic of Albania in the late 1940s, and the provision of mercenaries and supplies to the royalist rebels in North Yemen after 1962.
16. Both the US strategic hamlets in Vietnam and the Portuguese *aldeamentos* in Mozambique, were modelled on the New Villages of the Malayan campaign. The Rhodesian policy of 'Protected Villages' along the Mozambique border is also similar. Another means by which this technology and experience is diffused is via the training at British institutions of military personnel from ex-colonies. For example, the Sandhurst register of officers who 'passed out' in March 1973 included personnel from the following countries: Abu Dhabi, Bahrain, Botswana, Brunei, Dubai, Gibraltar, Ghana, Iran, Iraq, Jamaica, Kenya, Malawi, Malaysia, Nepal, Nigeria, Oman, Qatar, Saudi Arabia, Sierra Leone, Singapore, Thailand, United Arab Amirates, Uganda, Zaire. In written Answers to a Parliamentary Question, the British Minister of Defence stated on 23 February 1976 that British personnel have been serving with 33 other armies in the previous five years, and that a total of 2,250 serving members of 66 foreign countries were at that time undergoing training in Britain. While not all of these were involved in counter-insurgency training, there can be no doubt that British experience in this domain is being widely diffused to selected personnel from many other armies. (See Appendix I).
17. See Philip Darby, *British Defence Policy East of Suez, 1947-1968,* London 1973, pp. 130-33. Frank Kitson describes his experiences in this war in *Bunch of Fives* (London, 1977).
18. D. L. Price, *Oman: Insurgency and Development,* London, 1975, pp.. 11-12.
19. Robert Thompson, *Defeating Communist Insurgency,* London, 1966, p. 123.
20. Kennedy Trevaskis, *Shades of Amber,* London, 1968, p. 208.
21. *Les Emirates Mirages,* Paris 1975, pp 96-97.
22. *Report of the Committee of Privy Counsellors Appointed to Consider Authorized Procedures for the Interrogation of Persons Suspected of Terrorism,* Cmnd. 4901, March 1972, p. 3.

Appendix I

The following extract is from *Hansard*, House of Commons, London.

Friday 20 February 1976
Mr. Stanley Newens (Labour/Co-operative) (Harlow)

2. Mr. Newens — To ask the Secretary for Defence, if he will list the states which have serving members of their armed forces currently undergoing training in Great Britain; and if he will list the numbers in each case.

Answer — (Mr. Roy Mason) At the end of January 1976 serving members of the armed forces of the following countries were undergoing training in Great Britain:

ALGERIA	LEBANON
ARGENTINE	LIBYA
AUSTRALIA	MALAWI
BANGLADESH	MALAYSIA
BARBADOS	MAURITIUS
BELGIUM	NEPAL
BRAZIL	NETHERLANDS
BRUNEI	NEW ZEALAND
BURMA	NIGERIA
CANADA	NORWAY

CHILE	OMAN
DENMARK	PAKISTAN
ECUADOR	PERU
EIRE	PHILLIPINES
EGYPT	PORTUGAL
FRANCE	QATAR
GAMBIA	SAUDI ARABIA
WEST GERMANY	SIERRA LEONE
GHANA	SINGAPORE
GREECE	SRI LANKA
GUYANA	SUDAN
HONG KONG	SWEDEN
INDIA	SWITZERLAND
INDONESIA	THAILAND
IRAN	TONGA
IRAQ	TRINIDAD AND TOBAGO
ISRAEL	TURKEY
ITALY	UNITED ARAB EMIRATES
JAMAICA	UNITED STATES OF AMERICA
JAPAN	VENEZUELA
JORDAN	YEMEN
KENYA	ZAIRE
KUWAIT	ZAMBIA

The number involved in such training was about 2,250.

Ministry of Defence
23 February, 1976

*   *   *

Thursday 19 February 1976
Mr. Stanley Newens (Labour/Co-operative) (Harlow)

77. *Mr. Newens* — To ask the Secretary of State for Defence, if he will list all the foreign armed forces in which members of Her Majesty's armed forces are

known to be currently serving; and if he will give the number in each case.

78. *Mr. Newens* — To ask the Secretary of State for Defence, if he will list all the foreign armed forces to which members of Her Majesty's armed forces have been assigned or seconded over the course of the last five years; and if he will give the number involved in each case.

Answer — (Mr. Roy Mason) Over the past five years members of Her Majesty's armed forces have served abroad on loan, in exchange posts, or as members of British Service training and advisory teams with the armed forces of a number of foreign and Commonwealth countries. The following table lists the countries concerned, the numbers involved at 31st December of each year, and the numbers currently serving.

Ministry of Defence
23 February, 1976

Numbers at Year Ended 31 December:

	1971	1972	1973	1974	1975	Currently Serving
AUSTRALIA	159	120	136	107	89	86
BERMUDA	4	4	4	4	4	4
BRUNEI	52	49	58	64	90	90
CANADA	96	88	90	87	82	76
FIJI	-	-	1	-	-	-
FRANCE	7	7	7	7	8	8
FR GERMANY	4	4	6	11	14	14
GHANA	1	-	-	-	-	-
INDIA	1	-	-	-	-	-
ITALY	-	1	1	3	1	1
IRAN	21	48	36	62	71	74

JAMAICA	1	-	-	-	-	-
KENYA	104	28	14	31	18	18
KUWAIT	106	112	112	118	118	118
LIBYA	71	14	-	-	-	-
MALAWI	29	22	19	4	-	-
MALAYSIA	209	165	87	51	19	16
NEPAL	1	1	1	1	1	1
NETHERLANDS	7	9	9	10	10	10
NEW ZEALAND	4	5	7	9	7	7
NIGERIA	12	9	7	3	-	7
NORWAY	2	2	2	2	2	2
OMAN	92	121	154	170	235	216
PAKISTAN	1	1	1	1	1	1
PERU	-	8	-	-	2	2
QATAR	-	-	-	1	8	8
SAUDI ARABIA	6	5	6	6	6	6
SINGAPORE	79	91	89	42	13	13
SOUTH AFRICA	1	1	1	1	1	1
SUDAN	-	5	6	9	8	8
UNION OF ARAB EMIRATES	121	105	77	53	43	44
UNITED STATES OF AMERICA	137	154	186	191	191	195
ZAIRE		9	9	-	-	-

Appendix II

Correspondence on Oman between the Gulf Committee and Prime Minister Harold Wilson, 1975.

Dear Mr. Wilson,

Today we are demonstrating* in order to express our opposition to your government's policies in the state of Oman. Your government has continued the policy of its Conservative predecessor, and is providing considerable assistance to the Sultan of Oman in his brutal attempt to crush all dissent in his country. By providing military personnel and equipment to the Sultan, the Labour government is perpetuating an autocratic system of government and is enabling that system to impose itself on those who are trying to build a different and free Oman.

The Labour Party is committed to opposing colonialism in southern Africa, and, as numerous members of your own Party have now pointed out, this pledge is inconsistent with a continued British commitment to Oman. Last December, eighty-seven Members of Parliament, most of them from the Labour Party, supported a motion calling on the government to reconsider its policy in the Sultanate, and pointed out that the Defence Review provides a suitable context for such a reconsideration. We hope that you will take note of this suggestion, and we urge you and your colleagues to end British participation in the Sultan's campaigns. Only when all foreign troops have left Oman, and when those imprisoned for political dissent have been released, will the Omani people be able to decide freely their own future.

Yours sincerely,

The Gulf Committee

*This letter was handed in to 10 Downing Street during a demonstration against the British intervention in Oman, organised by the Iranian Students Society in Britain, the Palestine Yemen-Gulf Solidarity Committee, and the Gulf Committee

*   *   *

To: The Gulf Committee, 6 Endsleigh Street,
London WC1
25 March 1975

Gentlemen,
Your letter of 9 March to the Prime Minister has been passed on to me to answer.

We do not accept your basic premise that Her Majesty's Government are assisting the Sultan of Oman 'in his brutal attempt to crush all dissent in his country'. Her Majesty's Government provide assistance to the Sultan of Oman, a sovereign state with which we enjoy friendly relations, against a professionally-organised and externally-supported armed subversive movement which threatens the stability of the area. There is no conflict here between the opposition of the Labour

Party to all forms of colonialism and Her Majesty's Government's present policy towards Oman. Under the present Sultan, Oman is making great social and economic advances for the benefit of the people and Her Majesty's Government believe it is right to give this development every encouragement. As the Defence Review clearly states, in these circumstances Her Majesty's Government do not think it would be right to make any changes in the present arrangements we have with Oman.

Yours sincerely,

J. T. M. Lucas, Middle East Department, Foreign and Commonwealth Office, London SW1

*   *   *

To: The Prime Minister, 10 Downing Street,
London SW1
26 April 1975

Dear Mr Wilson,

We wrote to you on 9 March of this year concerning British policy towards the Sultanate of Oman, and have since received in reply a letter from Mr. J. T. M. Lucas of the Middle East Department of the Foreign Office.

Mr. Lucas' letter fails to answer any of the substantive points raised in our original communication, and in addition alleges certain points about Oman that we consider to be quite false. He says that your Government does not accept our charge that it is helping the Sultan of Oman 'in his brutal attempt to crush all dissent in his country', yet he provides no argument or evidence to deny either that the Sultan's policies are brutal or that they are designed to crush all dissent. This week's announcement that the Sultan's court's have sentenced four members of the opposition to death is relevant in this respect, as is the singular failure of the Sultan to alter in any way the autocratic political system inherited from his father.

Mr. Lucas alleges that Oman is 'a sovereign state', when this is no more than a legal piety. Every independent observer, and many more who were not so independent, to have visited Oman in recent years has attested to the fact that the government of that country is dependent for its survival on foreign military aid, and that the most important economic and military personnel in the country are nationals of foreign states. Moreover, Mr. Lucas justifies British intervention on the grounds that the opposition is 'professionally-organised and externally-supported'. Would Her Majesty's Government have a different policy if the opposition was made up of amateurs? And is it not the case that it is the Sultans of Oman who have been 'externally-supported', indeed supported by Britain, since the early nineteenth century?

Mr. Lucas' cosmetic description of the economic changes as being 'for the benefit of the people' hardly accords with the known facts of recent months. An estimated half of the Sultan's revenues is being spent in pursuing the Dhofar war, and the monarch himself has spent considerable sums on luxurious consumption — whether £18,000 on perfume in Harrods, £30 millions on a luxury yacht, and an unknown amount purchasing Hitler's former Bavarian retreat.

We therefore reaffirm our view that British intervention in Omin is inconsistent with the Labour Party's claim to oppose colonialism, and that Britain is helping to perpetuate an autocracy by pursuing such a policy.

Yours sincerely,

The Gulf Committee

*   *   *

To: The Gulf Committee, 6 Endsleigh Street,
London WC1
13 May 1975

Dear Sir,

Your letter of 26 April to the Prime Minister has been passed to me for answer.

I note that your interpretation of events is different from that of Her Majesty's Government as outlined in Mr. Lucas' reply of 25 March to your letter of 9 March. As you may have noticed, however, the Defence Secretary visited Oman in April, and, after talks with the Oman Government and military leaders and a visit to Dhofar, reaffirmed that Britain would continue its military assistance to Oman, which he described as a friendly ally, in its war against the rebels.

There seems to be little meeting ground between our viewpoints but I hope that this further letter will at least have made Her Majesty's Goverment's position clear to you.

Yours sincerely,

Patrick Wright, Private Secretary, 10 Downing Street

Appendix III

Facsimile reproduction of phychological warfare leaflet used by the British in Oman in the 1960's.

'If you see anyone burying a mine or hear of a person burying a mine'.

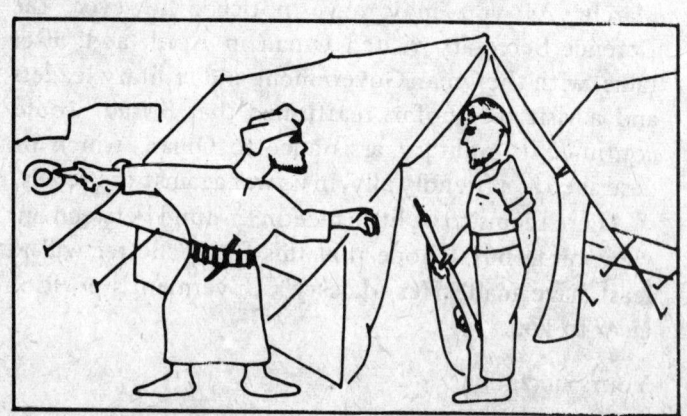

'Inform the nearest army camp'.

MERCENARIES

'Show them the place where the mine is buried so that they can pick it up'.

'You will be given 700 rials'.

The following advert appeared in the 2nd October 1975 issue of Flight International.

THE SULTANATE OF OMAN

Helicopter Pilots

There are continuing requirements for operational Helicopter Pilots in the Air Force of the Sultanate of Oman. Applicants must be ex-British Armed Forces, up to the age of 45, with *recent* military flying experience and have at least 1,000 hours on rotary wing aircraft.

These are contract appointments (initially for 3 years, renewable by mutual agreement), carrying the rank of Flight Lieutenant on engagement, and are unaccompanied although facilities exist for short family visits. Conditions of service are attractive including annual emoluments commencing at the equivalent of £8,200 (tax free) single air conditioned mess type accommodation and services provided free, an end of contract gratuity and generous home leave with air passages paid.

Apply with brief details to Box No. 9349, Flight International, Dorset House, Stamford Street, London SE1 9LU.